Six Phases

of

Discipleship

By

Rachel Armstead

Unless otherwise stated, all scripture quotations are from The Authorized (King James) Version. Rights in the Authorized Version in the United Kingdom are vested in the Crown. Reproduced by permission of the Crown's patentee, Cambridge University Press. Scripture quotations taken from the Contemporary English Version Copyright © 1991, 1992, 1995 by American Bible Society. Used by Permission. Scripture quotations marked (NIV) are taken from the Holy Bible, New International Version®, NIV®. Copyright © 1973, 1978, 1984, 2011 by Biblica, Inc.™ Used by permission of Zondervan. All rights reserved worldwide. www.zondervan.com The "NIV" and "New International Version" are trademarks registered in the United States Patent and Trademark Office by Biblica, Inc.™ Scripture quotations marked (NLT) are taken from the Holy Bible, New Living Translation, copyright © 1996, 2004, 2007 by Tyndale House Foundation. Used by permission of Tyndale House Publishers, Inc., Carol Stream, Illinois 60188. All rights reserved. Scripture quotation taken from the Amplified Bible, Copyright © 1954, 1958, 1962, 1964, 1965, 1987 by The Lockman Foundation. Used by permission.

ISBN: 0-692-61255-6
ISBN-13: 978-0-692-61255-6

DEDICATION

This book is dedicated to my wonderful mother, Rev. Hattie Miller.

Thank you for your countless prayers, unconditional love, and training me up in the way I should go.

CONTENTS

Introduction

There is no negating the power and influence that flows from a great leader. Throughout the history of mankind, the world has known many leaders who have demonstrated great power and influence over all who followed them. There have been leaders in politics, religion, the sciences, as well as simple social causes. These leaders have made significant contributions during their lifetime and have paved the way for those who would come after them. While these leaders may have been imperfect men and women, full of mistakes and shortcomings, they were effective in their leadership positions.

The Bible records the deeds of remarkable leaders, chosen and used by God, such as Moses, King David, and the Apostle Paul. I wholeheartedly believe that Jesus Christ was the world's Greatest Leader. His life, wisdom, teachings, and self-sacrifice were and are currently extraordinary. The example of leadership displayed through the life of Christ is exemplary. Jesus is the Son of God; by nature He is perfect and sinless. He is a leader who has unconditional love for all mankind. He loves those who follow Him and those who hate Him. Jesus demonstrated love in His life as well as in His death. The best part of it all: unlike other leaders who have lived and long ago died, Jesus rose from the dead three days after His death. He is alive today, leading any and all who will allow Him to be Lord and Savior of their life. Who in their right mind would pass up an opportunity to follow the world's greatest leader?

Prior to one becoming a successful leader there must be a time of learning and preparation. In *Six Phases of Discipleship* we will see what Jesus taught and modeled, additional scriptures that expound upon these principles, and personal application for all of these phases in our lives today as modern day disciples of Jesus Christ:

1. Relationship   *2. Discipline*   *3. Prayer*

4. Stewardship   *5. Humility*   *6. Authority*

Phase 1: Relationship

It is interesting that Jesus did not go into the synagogue and pick out the top twelve religious leaders as disciples. Jesus was the Son of God so why didn't He go to those who were already studying the law of God in the temple on a daily basis? That was not God's plan. At the temple He could find many studying about the law and religious matters. When Jesus started His earthly ministry He went to the seashore and called fishermen to follow Him, and later chose a cheating tax collector. Here we see the Sovereignty of God; choosing specific people who He wanted to fulfill His will. God's ways are so much higher than our ways and His thoughts so much higher than our thoughts.[1] These men were not perfect, but God loved them and instructed Jesus to choose them in spite of their character weaknesses, their heart condition, past mistakes and failures, and all of the mistakes and failures to come.

A disciple by one definition is *a person who believes in the ideas of a leader, especially a religious or political one and tries to live according to those ideas* (Cambridge, n.d). When each of the disciples was called, they all had to make a choice as to whether or not they would follow Jesus. Peter and Andrew were fishermen on their boat working when Jesus called them. Jesus promised to make them "fishers of men."[2] James and John were on a boat working alongside their father mending fishing nets, when Jesus called them; they immediately left the ship and their father, and followed Him.[3]

I love to read about the call of Levi, also known as Matthew, the publican or tax collector. "And after these things he went forth, and saw a publican, named Levi, sitting at the receipt of custom: and he said unto him, Follow me. And he left all, rose up, and followed him (Luke 5:27-28)." Tax collectors were known for being evil because they cheated their people, the Jews, out of their money. When Jesus called Levi he was working, but he willingly left all he had. Levi went a step further in throwing a great feast prior to leaving, inviting many of his tax-collector friends and associates. The scribes and Pharisees were shocked to see that Jesus and his disciples chose to eat and drink with tax-collectors and sinners. Jesus responded wisely by saying "I came not to call the righteous, but sinners to repentance."[4] Jesus was popular, performed many miracles, and was a phenomenal teacher; so it was to be expected that He would have a lot of followers. Many people thought He was the Messiah and were glad to be His disciple. Unfortunately, when Jesus began to teach about being the Bread of Life things took a different turn. We see it in the book of John chapter six: "From that time many of his disciples went back, and walked no more with him. Then said Jesus to the twelve, Will ye also go away? Then Simon Peter answered him, Lord, to whom shall we go? Thou hast the words of eternal life. And we believe and are sure that thou art that Christ, the Son of the living God (John 6:66-69)."

At any time the chosen twelve disciples could have turned and walked away from Jesus. Some of the other disciples chose that path during Jesus' earthly ministry. Jesus personally taught, trained, and cared for His disciples. They established and developed a close relationship because He spent countless hours with them. The disciples willingly followed Him and spent many hours sitting at His feet to learn all they could. They spent three and half years learning about Christ and the Kingdom of God so that they could be equipped to spend the rest of their lives teaching others about Christ and the Kingdom of God. The option to stop following Jesus was never taken away from them. That is why we are able to read about Judas' betrayal of Christ. His decision to turn away from following Jesus ultimately led to the tragic loss of his life.[5]

As a born again believer, you always have a choice. At any time you are able to exercise your "freewill." God has no prisoners in His Kingdom. A disciple must be willing to follow the instruction and commands of their teacher. This is done out of devotion and sincere commitment to learning. True disciples will go wherever and do whatever their teacher requires of them. All disciples are required to exercise faith in the knowledge, skill, and ability of their teacher. As children of the Most High God, we confidently know that the Teacher we are following has all knowledge and power; yet we still must walk by faith and not by sight.[6]

Your faith becomes stronger as you learn about God and develop an intimate relationship with Him. This is a relationship that will last for eternity. Like all relationships, a walk with God is going to require something of you. In Mark 8:34, Jesus put it this way: "Whosoever will come after me, let him deny himself, and take up his cross, and follow me." Just in case there is some doubt as to what is being required, take a look at how the Amplified Bible explains this verse: "If anyone desires to be My disciple, let him deny himself [disregard, lose sight of, and] forget himself and his own interests] and take up his cross and follow Me [cleave steadfastly to Me, conform wholly to My example in living and, if need be, in dying, also]. You must be willing to give your life and your heart to the Lord. If you take a moment to truly think about it, you have nothing else to offer unto the Lord other than your heart and your time.

"It's up to you to fan the flames of your relationship with the Lord."

During the first phase of discipleship you have the personal encounter, or meeting with Christ. This is the birth of the relationship. At that meeting Christ offers a fresh start and a better way of life. Jesus said "No man can come to me, except the Father which hath sent me draw him (John 6:44)." No one wakes up one day and decides to give their life to Christ. No, the Spirit of God must draw them to Him. God does the drawing and also gives you the desire for Him, but leaves the ultimate decision to enter into covenant relationship with Him up to you. You must choose to act on the desire that God places within you. The Amplified Bible says it this way, "No one is able to come unto Me unless the Father Who sent Me attracts and draws him and gives him the desire to come to Me (John 6:44)."

Many people hope to have a personal relationship with Jesus Christ, "someday." Too many people think they have time to reject Christ now and accept Him sometime later in life. They can feel His power and love drawing them every time they hear the gospel being preached or taught but fail to follow through with yielding and surrendering their life to Christ. Others will go to church, ask for prayer or listen to Christian or Gospel music hoping that will satisfy the spiritual void. There is no substitute for God or His Presence in your life. "Today if ye will hear his voice, harden not your hearts (Heb. 4:7)." Today is the best day to start, have and maintain a personal relationship with Jesus Christ. You would be wise to answer and surrender to God the day and moment that He calls and draws you to Himself. Tomorrow is not promised to anyone. Jesus freely gives forgiveness of sin and eternal life to whoever believes on Him.[7] In exchange, believe in your heart and confess with your mouth that Jesus is the Son of God and invite Him to be both Lord and Savior of your life.[8] That is to get you started on the path of relationship and discipleship. When developing a relationship, a healthy one, three things will eventually happen: learning, sharing, and growing. The relationship grows as both parties take time to learn about and share with each other.

There are many ways to look at how you can grow and develop a personal relationship with God. As a Christian you will learn about God as you read and study His Word, and you can share your life with Him as you spend time in prayer, praise and worship, and through your church attendance and fellowship with other born-again believers. Perhaps you are a born again Christian and have been for quite some time. You are following after Christ and doing your best to be one of His present-day disciples. We have all experienced the new burning desire to learn about God. The excitement about going to church and anticipation for Bible study are common for new Believers. After a while the fire of excitement can be smothered and perhaps even go out completely. It's up to you to fan the flames of your relationship with the Lord. There is power, fire, and excitement in the Kingdom of God! Jesus wasn't boring and I'm sure His disciples weren't bored following Him. Everyday there was opportunity to impact the lives of others through teaching, healing, deliverance, fellowship, and acts of love. Those same opportunities are available for you today.

Think of the examples of how Jesus impacted lives in natural settings. He attended a wedding, and had an established friendship with Lazarus, and his two sisters, Mary and Martha, and he visited their home. In addition, there are the miracles Jesus performed such as healing the sick, walking on water and raising up the dead. And to think, Jesus told His disciples they would also do great things. There's no time for your fire to go out as present-day disciples. Now is the time to strengthen and feed your relationship with the Lord. "Draw nigh to God, and he will draw nigh to you (James 4:8)." Spend more time in His Word, reading and studying. Spend more time in His presence, worshipping and praying. Spend more time sharing the love of Christ with the rest of the world. I challenge you now to revisit your salvation experience. Take a stroll down memory lane from the earlier days of your new birth in Christ and examine your relationship with the Lord today.

Remember, God chose you because He already knew that you would choose Him.[9] He knew that you would love Him, serve Him, and pursue after a close relationship with Him. God has blessings ready to be released upon all who are in covenant relationship with Him.

Questions for discussion/reflection:

1. What words would you use to describe your relationship with The Lord?

2. What efforts are made on your part to maintain and further develop a healthy intimate relationship with The Lord?

Disciple's Discovery Scriptures

"Phase 1: Relationship"

[1]Isa. 55:9   [2]Matt. 4:19   [3]Matt. 4:22

[4]Luke 5:32   [5]Matt. 27:3-5   [6]2 Cor. 5:7

[7]John 3:16; 1 John 1:9   [8]Rom. 10:9   [9]Eph. 1:4

Phase 2: Discipline

The second phase of discipleship is discipline. A lot of things come to mind whenever I hear the word "discipline." I immediately think of punishment, correction, and strict enforcement of rules. Those things are true. For this section, I have chosen the following definition which I believe best fits within the context of discipleship: "training expected to produce a specific character or pattern of behavior, esp. training that produces moral or mental improvement (American Heritage, 1997)."

People often assume that Jesus was perfect while here on the earth and it is impossible to be anything like Him. That's not correct at all. Jesus came to the earth and was a living example of how children of God should live. He was a model for all age groups. As a child, He was obedient to His parents. At age 12, Jesus sat at the feet of the leaders in the temple learning and asking questions about the law of God.[10] As a young man, He learned how to be a carpenter working underneath His earthly father Joseph. This shows that Jesus had a job prior to starting His earthly ministry. Employment can be used as a tool for teaching discipline and responsibility. When He entered into full time ministry, Jesus spent a great deal of time teaching and ministering directly to the needs of the people through healing and deliverance. He did not say or do anything without God's approval and anointing. Jesus put it this way: "The words that I speak unto you I speak not of myself: but the Father that dwelleth in me, he doeth the works (John 14:10)."

Jesus modeled discipline through His everyday living and teaching. He chose disciples, who were not known to be Bible scholars so Jesus spent a lot of time teaching them. The disciples started at square one with Jesus and had to develop a discipline to remain at His feet, listening to His sermons and parables. There were times when He would have to re-teach the disciples privately because they didn't understand what He was teaching. Jesus was glad to explain things further to them.[11] The disciples had informal Bible study sessions with the greatest Teacher ever to walk the earth. Jesus also happens to be the Living Word.[12] Jesus was planting a seed in them, so that after His departure, the disciples would continue studying, learning, growing, and instructing future leaders and teachers in the making. It was important that they had a clear understanding of the Word of God and what exactly God was requiring of them. The disciples had a lot to learn in a short amount of time so there was nonstop teaching and on-the-job training by their Rabbi (Teacher), Jesus Christ. Jesus taught and modeled how to interact with people from all walks of life. He extended love, compassion, healing and forgiveness to adults as well as children; to the rich as well as the poor; and to the Jews as well as the non-Jews.

The disciples were committed to Jesus during His years of popularity, as well as when it became public knowledge that the Jews wanted to kill Him. It's one thing to have a level of commitment when things are going well and another thing altogether when your commitment gets put to the test through persecution, adversity, hardship, pain and suffering. A disciple must be a devoted follower, and devotion requires discipline. The disciples, who later became the Apostles in the book of Acts, would experience a level of persecution they had not yet come to understand. A true disciple will follow in both the good times and in the bad and prove their devotion. On several occasions, during their time of learning discipline, Jesus sent the disciples out to practice that which they had been learning. They were sent into towns to preach repentance, heal the sick and cast out devils.[13]

After His death and resurrection, Jesus returned to His disciples and gave them their final divine assignment, known as "The Great Commission." The disciples were instructed to go and "teach all nations, baptizing them in the name of the Father, and the Son, and of the Holy Ghost: teaching them to observe all things whatsoever I have commanded you: and lo, I am with you always, even unto the end of the world (Matt. 28:19-20)."

Jesus also taught principles that needed to be put into practice on a daily basis for the true child of God. He presented kingdom principles in Matthew chapters 5-7. Jesus explained that the disciples are now called to be the "salt of the earth" and the "light of the world."[14] They could no longer blend in and do whatever everyone else was doing. They were being called to a higher standard of living and a holy standard of living which would require discipline.

In the Kingdom of God, you have to do things God's way. There is no other option and there are no exceptions. Jesus truly practiced all that He preached! He only did those things that pleased the Father.[15] Jesus modeled disciplined obedience through His everyday living and teaching. Obedience is not automatic; it is in our nature to want to do whatever we want, whenever we want. You can call this the "Adamic nature." The Bible tells us that Jesus didn't live His life that way. "Though he were a Son, Jesus learned obedience through the things that he suffered (Heb. 5:8)." Disobedience does not work in the Kingdom of God. God has a standard of righteousness and holiness that cannot be compromised. Obedience is a mandate, not an option. God does not expect perfection; He knows we are human and limited but He does expect obedience. Jesus showed us that obedience to God is possible.

"Obedience to God is a mandate, not an option." Jesus forewarned His disciples that in this world they will have tribulation.[16] The word for tribulation in the Greek is "thlipsis" meaning "pressure" (Strong, 1890). Pressure will be applied as you endeavor to live a disciplined life for Christ. In the book of Acts, you can read about the persecution and suffering that the early church and Apostles had to endure simply for preaching the gospel of Jesus Christ. Despite it all, it's also encouraging reading about their determination and tenacity to keep preaching and praising God for the privilege of suffering for Christ.[17]

Being obedient to God will require that you practice self-denial and refuse to give in to what your flesh wants to do. This is demonstrated by Jesus in the Garden of Gethsemane. He was about to come face to face with His purpose and destiny: the cross. Jesus knew it would be physically brutal, emotionally draining, and the hardest thing He would have to do in His lifetime here on earth. The Bible says, "Being in agony he prayed more earnestly."[18] The natural man had Him pray again and ask God, in essence, if there were any other possible way for mankind to be redeemed and saved. But the spirit man added to each of the three prayers: "nevertheless, not my will, but thine be done."[19]

Our daily walk with the Lord is a walk of discipline and learning. The instruction needed to fully develop a life disciplined to the will and service of the Kingdom of God can only come through the Word of God. Each time you read the Bible, you can think of it as your time to sit at the feet of Jesus to learn as the disciples were able to do with Him. This reiterates the importance of learning and studying the Word of God. One of the greatest areas of discipline for the believer to establish is learning the Word of God. David put it this way: "Thy word have I hid in my heart that I might not sin against thee (Ps. 119:11)." Through the Word of God you can learn about God and what He offers to you as a born-again believer; you can also learn about the responsibilities of being a son/daughter of the Most High God.

In John 14:15, Jesus said, "If you love me, keep my commandments." Your love for God can be no greater than your obedience to God. It comes down to how you are living and quoting scripture is not enough. Although you may never memorize a lot of scriptures or understand every single bible verse, God expects you to live and walk daily in the truth that you do know and understand. You are to be responsible and expose ourselves to good biblical teaching and instruction through means such as attending a Bible study, Sunday school, or perhaps even a bible class at a college. Obedience is doing what God tells you to do and refusing to do what He tells you NOT to do. You have to do more than go to church, sing in the choir, serve on the usher board, give offerings, and compliment the pastor on the good sermon. To be obedient you must also walk in love and forgiveness towards those who treat you badly.

"Remember, it is sin to know what you ought to do and then not do it (James 4:17, NLT)." Our obedience to God includes even the smallest detail of our lives.

Through spiritual discipline and God's grace, you can be a disciple in the earth helping to expand the Kingdom of God. We learn the golden rule at an early age "Do to others as you would have them do to you (Luke 6:31, NIV)." But in current times we add, "When it's convenient and others are watching." God is always watching and He sees what is going on in your heart at all times. As you set your heart and mind to become a disciplined servant, make pleasing God your number one focus. As God's disciple, you can study and learn His Word and what He is requiring of you, but it means nothing if you are not willing to obey and apply all that you learn.

Questions for discussion/reflection:

1. Discipline is training to produce character. What actions can you take to become more disciplined spiritually?

2. What are some consequences of *obedience* to God **AND** *disobedience* to God? (It's important to know both!)

Disciple's Discovery Scriptures

"Phase 2: Discipline"

[10]Luke 2:46-47   [11]Mark 4:3   [12]John 1:1,14

[13]Matt. 10:1   [14]Matt. 5:13-14   [15]John 8:29

[16]John 6:35   [17]Acts 5:40-42   [18]Luke 22:44

[19]Luke 22:42

Phase 3: Prayer

I have always defined prayer as "communication with God." My personal definition generically describes prayer as a casual event that may or may not take place with any sort of regularity. Christian Apologetics and Research Ministry (CARM) defined prayer as *"a privilege and an obligation of the Christian where we communicate with God.* The use of the words "privilege and obligation" are what stood out to me - prayer is a privilege and an obligation. Consistent and honest communication are the backbones for any relationship, whether it be a friendship, romantic relationship, or a working relationship. For the born-again believer, prayer is a vital necessity in your walk with the Lord. You cannot be a true disciple for the Lord and not have ongoing communication with Him. You can search the scriptures and see that Jesus spent a lot of time in prayer.[20]

"When it comes to prayer, quitting is not an option."

You may wonder why "prayer" is included as a phase of discipleship. Every relationship requires ongoing communication. Prayer is an essential part of discipleship because it is the way in which we communicate with God and also a time when He can communicate with us. Through ongoing communication, relationships are able to develop and grow. The disciples left their livelihoods, their families and friends, and dedicated the rest of their lives to following Jesus. They made a commitment, and the process of learning what was needed to be a true disciple of Christ would be a work in progress. Each day was filled with invaluable lessons, one of which was prayer.

Jesus often took time away from the crowds to pray and commune with His Father (Mark 1:35). Those private times of prayer helped prepare Him for those public times of prayer and ministry. I can imagine the disciples took note of how often He prayed and how long He prayed. Jesus must have done it with such frequency that the disciples were able to conclude prayer is important and asked Him to teach them how to pray. Jesus knew that prayer was not a light issue or something to do because you see someone else doing it. Jesus taught lessons on prayer and then became a model for His disciples.[21] Prior to starting His ministry, I think we can safely assume that Jesus spent time praying when He spent forty days fasting in the wilderness.

What would you do if you knew in a few hours you would be arrested, unfairly judged, beaten, and soon after dead?

Why did Jesus pray so much and so often? This is a question I asked myself. Was it really necessary for Jesus, of all people, to spend so much time praying? Absolutely! Jesus did not do anything that was unnecessary for Him or for us. I have come to understand that because He was the Son of God He needed to communicate with His Father. He came down from heaven where He had been living in eternity with God. Jesus was present in the beginning when the world was created. Now that He had taken on human form and was physically present on earth as a man, Jesus needed God's wisdom and guidance as never before. He was used to being in constant communication with His Father. One can only wonder how long it took before the disciples asked Jesus to teach them how to pray. Prayer was one of the most important lessons that Jesus would teach. He taught them how to communicate with God for themselves. On the day of Pentecost the church was birthed as a result of prayer.[22]

During His ministry, Jesus prayed and the sick were healed, blinded eyes were opened, and the dead came back to life. He prayed and fed five thousand men with two fish and five loaves of bread. Down to the final days of His life, Jesus maintained a strong prayer life and taught about the importance of prayer. He prayed before His arrest and crucifixion in the Garden of Gethsemane. What would you do if you knew in a few hours you would be arrested, unfairly judged, beaten, and soon after dead? Jesus did not whine and complain, have a wild party, or demand that God change what He already knew to be God's will for His life. He chose the best option available, prayer.

Jesus prayed because this was an issue with which no other human being could help Him. God either had to change the situation or change Jesus in the situation. Jesus tried to get His disciples to join Him in prayer, but they were too tired and fell asleep.[23] The disciples did not fully understand that they were hours away from witnessing the most important event in the history of mankind: Jesus dying on a cross for the sins of the world. God moved on behalf of the prayer His Son offered to Him: "And there appeared an angel unto him from heaven, strengthening him (Luke 22:43)." It is amazing how God is able to hear our cry and petition and provide exactly what we need, especially when we do not know what to pray. When you have a heart to do the will of the Lord, God will make sure you have everything you need to do it!

During one of His many lessons, Jesus spoke and expounded on the importance of prayer. "And he spake a parable unto them to this end, that men ought always to pray, and not to faint (Luke 18:1)." Jesus spoke a parable about a woman who went to a judge for help dealing with her enemies. The judge initially ignored her request but eventually got weary of her persistence and decided to move on her behalf so she would stop bothering him. Jesus was illustrating that if an unjust man can be moved by persistent petitions, how much more will our Heavenly Father move on behalf of those who are praying to Him with faith and persistence? When it comes to prayer, quitting is not an option. You cannot stop praying for your loved ones simply because you see no change in their lives. You can't stop praying for healing because you see no change in physical health. You cannot afford to quit talking to your Heavenly Father.

How many times have you made costly mistakes due to failing to pray before doing something or making a life changing decision? You cannot make it in this world on your own, without divine help and protection from God. Pray and maintain ongoing communication with the Father so that He can have every opportunity to speak and communicate with you about His plans and His will. Regardless of how long it takes God to answer, continue to make your requests known unto God. It could be that God wants to give you peace in the midst of your situation as you patiently wait for Him to work things out. God does not want you to worry. The Apostle Paul gives us clear-cut instructions concerning worry. "Be careful for nothing (Phil 4:6)." Instead of worrying, make your petitions known to The Lord. Share the issue with The Lord in prayer. Seek His will and get His mind on the matter. As you give it to God, He gives you His peace. He will not force thoughts of peace into your mind; however, if you choose to trust Him, He will keep you in perfect peace.[24] Do not allow your mind to dwell constantly on your problems or issues. Worry and fear will try to come after you have given it all over into The Lord's hands. Thankfully, the Peace of God comes to guard (or to protect) your mind.

As disciples of Jesus Christ, there is a standard in place when we come to God in prayer. That standard can be summed up in three key words: forgiveness, faith, and focus. In Mark 11, Jesus cursed a fig tree and caused it to dry up from the roots overnight.[25] Because the disciples were amazed at this miracle Jesus turned this into a teachable moment for them to encourage their faith. He concluded by saying "Therefore I say unto you, What things soever ye desire, when you pray, believe that ye receive them and ye shall have them (Mark 11:24)." I am sure the disciples were pumped up and anxious to try this principle of praying, believing, and receiving. However, Jesus had a few more words to say on the subject of believing and receiving. "And when ye stand praying, forgive, if ye have ought against any; that your Father also which is in heaven may forgive you your trespasses. But if ye do not forgive, neither will your Father which is in heaven forgive your trespasses (Mark 11:25-26)." One moment Jesus is talking about faith in God, speaking to mountains, believing and receiving. The next moment, in my translation, He says, "Oh, and by the way, make sure your heart is right towards everyone when you start your faith-filled prayer to God!" I intentionally placed "forgiveness" as the first of the 3 F's to remember. Make sure that nothing hinders your prayers, including your refusal to forgive. When you do this, you are only hurting yourself. Keep your heart pure before the Lord and walk in forgiveness at all times. After forgiveness, you need faith to believe that God can handle your request.[26] We can have all the faith in the world and believe God for any and every thing, but if we do not have the love of God working in our hearts to the point that we forgive all others, then our faith means nothing. "Though I have all faith, so that I could remove mountains, and have not charity, I am nothing (1 Cor. 13:2)." As we align ourselves with the Word of God concerning forgiving all those who have trespassed against or offended us, then we can move on to the place of faith-filled prayers that yield results. Lastly, stay focused. Maintain your prayer focus even if the answer to your prayers seems to be delayed and you see no immediate change. Jesus put it this way: "And I say unto you, Ask, and it shall be given you; seek, and ye shall find; knock, and it shall be opened unto you. For every one that asketh receiveth; and he that seeketh findeth; and to him that knocketh it shall be opened (Luke 11:9-10)."

God has given us His Word that is forever settled in heaven, now you must daily choose to align your thoughts, actions, and your character to what is written. God will not give a favorable answer to ALL of your prayer requests. He is Sovereign and Omniscient; God does not have to give you an explanation when He decides not to answer one of your prayers or when His answer is "no."

If Jesus, the only begotten Son of God, spent much time praying to the Father, His disciples also need to spend time praying to the Father. Not all born-again believers know how to pray. I know many people who have been saved a long time that would rather not say a prayer in public because they lack confidence in their ability to pray. I, too, used to be that way. My prayer life improved as I prayed more and joined in prayer groups and services with more experienced Christians, who are referred to as "prayer warriors." These people can easily spend hours in prayer. When they finish praying, they have triumphed over the enemy, interceded for souls, released healing in bodies, and heard directly from the Lord. Every prayer warrior had to begin somewhere. If you are one who struggles in the area of prayer, you may consider starting a prayer journal or a prayer sheet on which you write down things and people you would like to pray about during your prayer time. You can later add to your list answered prayers and blessings recently received and then spend time thanking God for each thing on your list. In addition, set aside some quiet time where you allow God to speak to you. The more you pray, the more comfortable you become with praying and you will notice growth in your prayer life.

Ultimately, it is not about the length of the prayer that matters but rather the strength of your prayer. "The earnest prayer of a righteous person has great power and produces wonderful results (James 5:16, NLT)." If you find that your prayers are not producing any results, it may be time to do a re-examination of your heart and/or your relationship with the Lord.

Questions for discussion/reflection:

1. How can refusing to forgive effect your prayer life?

2. What impact can fear have on your prayer life?

Disciple's Discovery Scriptures

"Phase 3: Prayer"

[20]Matt. 14:23; Luke 5:1   [21]Matt. 6:6   [22]Acts 1:14; 2:1-2

[23]Matt. 26:41   [24]Isa. 26:3   [25]Mark 11:20   [26]Heb. 11:6

Phase 4: Stewardship

Stewardship is defined by Merriam-Webster as being *"the careful and responsible management of something entrusted to one's care."* When looking at the things that were entrusted into Jesus' care while He was here on earth, you can begin with His life. Jesus dedicated His life to doing the will of His Father. He took necessary steps to prepare Himself for the ministry He would start at the age of thirty. Jesus modeled good stewardship before He began ministry and before He called His first disciple to follow Him. Jesus attended the synagogue regularly and not only did He attend, He studied and asked questions to enhance His learning and knowledge.

Jesus was a carpenter, which means He took time to learn a skill and a trade in which He worked for at least ten years. I believe Jesus was dedicated as a carpenter, and put His best effort into every job. Jesus stated, "He that is faithful in that which is least, is faithful also in much (Luke 16:10)." If Jesus was not faithful to carry out the duties of a carpenter, I don't believe God would have committed to Him the job of training the future Apostles who would be instrumental in the birth of the church.

When it was time for Jesus to start His ministry, He was baptized by John the Baptist, and then the Spirit of God led Him on a wilderness journey. Jesus went on an eight week fast, which was accompanied by various temptations from the devil.[27] Here we have a glimpse of God's process for His stewards. God will require you to be faithful in a few areas before you can be anointed to do a great work for the Kingdom of God. Good stewardship must begin with you in your personal relationship with Him and in your daily life concerning your family, home, and/or your vocation. There should be careful management of all that has been given unto you.

Another area where you can see how Jesus was a good steward is through His responsibility of the twelve disciples. At the end of His ministry, Jesus told the Lord, "While I was with them in the world, I kept them in thy name: those that thou gavest me I have kept, and none of them is lost, but the son of perdition; that the scripture might be fulfilled (John 17:12)." Jesus was able to make this bold statement only because He knew He had exercised responsible stewardship. Jesus stated that He came to the earth to minister or serve, not be ministered unto (Mark 10:45). A steward is first and foremost a servant. Jesus came to the earth to serve and do the will of His Heavenly Father. As a disciple of Christ, you are called to be God's servant. "If any man serve me, let him follow; and where I am, there shall also my servant be: if any man serve me, him will my Father honour (John 12:26)." He led His disciples from city to city ministering and modeling how to show and share God's love with everyone. Jesus came to seek, save, and serve all people, from the social outcasts on up to the social elite. He asked for nothing in return as He ministered to everyone.

Jesus gave an impromptu lesson on good stewardship while feeding the multitude of 5000 men. After the disciples had served everyone, Jesus told them to gather up the leftovers.[28] Two lessons can be gleaned from this: gratitude and appreciation. As a steward, you must have an appreciation for that which God entrusts to your care. In this text, God provided abundance from very little food. The disciples were able to witness first-hand the power of God through this miracle. They saw that there truly is nothing too hard for God as five thousand men ate until they were filled and afterwards the disciples collected 12 baskets of leftovers. God provided as they gave out and served. In the end the disciples had way more than what they started with and for this they could be grateful. They now had plenty to appreciate and enjoy later.

Even in the face of opposition and blatant rejection, Jesus modeled good stewardship over His ministry. The disciples tried to deter Jesus by reminding Him that there were people who were seeking to take His life after He received the report of Lazarus' sickness; but Jesus knew that the will and purpose of God would prevail.[29] Jesus never spoke a word of fear; in fact He was always teaching and encouraging them in the area of their faith. Another example of modeling stewardship under opposition is when the storm arose on the lake and the disciples thought they would perish. In the moment, they woke Jesus and asked if He cared that they were about to perish.[30] Of course He cared! Jesus got up, rebuked the wind and spoke to the sea and simply said "Peace be still (Mark 4:39)." Jesus was a good steward over all those whom God had placed in His care, including Himself.

To further expound upon the topic of stewardship, let's consider Jesus' parable about the talents found in Matthew 25:14-30. A master goes into a far country, but before he leaves he distributes his goods to his three servants. The master knew his servants very well and each of them received talents, or money, according to their abilities. He was familiar with their work ethic, their strengths and limitations. After a while the master returns to see what the servants did with the talents that he entrusted into their care. The two servants who received five and two talents doubled theirs and received a favorable commendation from their master. The third servant, who was only given one talent, did not have a good report because he had not done anything with the one talent that the master had given to him. (Now we know why he was only given one talent!) He admitted to burying the talent, so he could give it back to the master upon his return. The master referred to him as a "wicked and slothful servant." The master commanded that the "unprofitable servant" be cast into outer darkness.

"Stewardship is taking a look at how we are caring for our body, soul, and spirit."

As the master knew his servants, God knows each of us. He knows our abilities as well as our limitations. God knew what gifts and talents would be best suited for us.[31] Some have been called to preach to the nations, while others have been gifted to serve only in the local church. The Contemporary English Version Bible says it well: "First, God chose some people to be apostles and prophets and teachers for the church. But he also chose some to work miracles or

25

heal the sick or help others or be leaders or speak different kinds of languages (1 Cor. 12:28)." You must find your place of service in the Kingdom of God.

In Matthew 25:33-40, Jesus taught about the kingdom of heaven. Those who will inherit the kingdom did not perform outrageous miracles nor were they classified as being great and powerful. They were regular people who showed the love of God to others through their actions. Today, these are the ones who feed the hungry, clothe the naked, take in the stranger, and visit the sick and those in prison. When you do these things, it is as if you are doing them unto Jesus Himself.[32] Many people in the Body of Christ are not called to be apostles, prophets, evangelists, pastors or teachers. You have been given the mandate to let your light shine and allow God to get glory out of all that you do.[33] You are to be good stewards of the light within you, which is the life of Christ.[34] We are all part of the Body, which is made up of many members.[35] No one is more important than another person in the eyes of God. We all have individual jobs to do. The enemy tries to get us to compete with one another in the Kingdom of God. We are all on the same team. It may seem that some jobs are greater than others, but you must remember that all stewards must be faithful at whatever job they are given. Whatever you decide to do, whether in the church or outside of the church, do it all for the Lord.[36]

What God may require of me, may be too much for you to handle and vice versa, so it would be best for you to simply do what you know God has given you to do. Do not do it for money, fame, or recognition; instead, do it because you love God and want to be a good steward over all that He has committed into your hands.

You can't talk about stewardship without talking about the "steward," which is you. God has hand-selected you for His purpose and His pleasure.[37] Stewardship is taking a look at how you are caring for your body, soul, and spirit. "Know ye not that ye are the temple of God, and that the Spirit of God dwelleth in you (1 Cor. 3:16)?" You are responsible for ensuring that your physical, mental, emotional, and spiritual needs get met. You only have one body to use in service for the Lord, so you must take care of it. Stewardship also requires that we give careful consideration to our reputation and our character. "Moreover, it is required in stewards, that a man be found faithful (1 Cor. 4:2)." This scripture requires us to take a closer look at our level of commitment in the Kingdom of God. Most successful CEO's are known for the strong work-ethic of putting in long hours on a regular basis. They are committed to the success of their business. Commit yourself to the success and growth of the Body of Christ and the winning of lost souls. Remain faithful to the task to which God has assigned you. Obey God regardless of what you or anyone else may think, say, or do. Two words can summarize the greatest qualities needed in a good steward: responsible and reliable. God called you, chose you, and anointed you to get the job done. Show up and do the work, be responsible. In the Kingdom of God there are no regular business hours, be reliable. God has invested a lot in you and someone needs the gift of God found in you today. Allow the Lord to get the glory out of your life as you serve Him.

Questions for discussion/reflection:

1. Do you serve others in the Kingdom of God? If so, how and when?

2. What specific steps do you take to properly care for your body, soul, and spirit?

Disciple's Discovery Scriptures

"Phase 4: Stewardship"

[27]Matt. 4:1-2   [28]John 6:12   [29]John 11:8

[30]Mark 4:38   [31]1 Cor. 12:18   [32]Matt. 25:37-40

[33]Matt. 5:16   [34]John 1:4   [35]1 Cor. 12:20

[36]Col. 3:23   [37]1 Pet. 2:9

Phase 5: Humility

Merriam-Webster defines humility as *"the quality or state of not thinking you are better than other people; the state of being humble."*[e] Humble by definition is *"marked by meekness or modesty in behavior, attitude, or spirit; not arrogant or prideful."* Jesus didn't come on the scene telling everyone to be humble. Instead, He gave practical instructions and directives that would require humility of heart if one chose to obey.

In Matthew chapter six, you will find a few of those practical instructions. Jesus told His disciples, when you give alms (offering), don't allow your left hand to see what your right hand is giving. Our offering is to be unto the Lord. This can include your monetary donations to the church, as well as anything that the Lord would ask you to give to someone in need. Jesus said that the hypocrites sound an alarm in the streets at the time of their giving so that they may have glory of men, and that's the full extent of their reward.

When you use discretion, your Father who sees in secret shall reward you openly.[38] God who sees all knows how to bless you for all to see. A little further in the same chapter, Jesus touches on the topic of fasting. There is no need to publicize the fact that you are fasting. The hypocrites have a sad countenance and disfigure their faces so everyone will know they are fasting. Fasting is a time of self-denial and putting one's focus on the things of God. It is personal and should not be exploited in any way to get glory or recognition for yourself. If you do, you will get nothing out of it, other than a few hunger pains. Jesus told them to anoint their head and wash their face.

In Luke 18, Jesus teaches on the topic of humility from another angle with a parable for those in His listening audience who "trusted in themselves that they were righteous, and despised others (v. 9)." He tells the story of two men going to the temple to pray, one was a religious leader, a Pharisee, and the other was a known sinner, a publican (tax collector). The Pharisee prayed a very judgmental prayer, even included a remark about the publican who was also at the temple. However the publican, who stood off by himself, didn't look up towards heaven, but beat his chest in sorrow confessing that he was a sinner and pleading for God's mercy. Jesus concludes by saying the sinner was the one who went home justified and that those who exalt themselves will be humbled, and those who humble themselves will be exalted (v.14).

I believe that the greatest teaching on humility that Jesus gave was when He taught on love. "You have heard that it hath been said, Thou shalt love thy neighbor and hate thine enemy. But I say unto you, Love your enemies, bless them that curse you, do good to them that hate you, and pray for them which despitefully use you, and persecute you (Matt. 5:43-44)." This type of love would require one to exercise great humility. It's easy to think you have a right to have an issue with someone who doesn't like you. Why should you spend time loving them, blessing them, and praying for them? Because Jesus said so! Somewhere along the way there must be a change of your heart and mind.

"Humility is a choice that each individual has to make on a daily basis."

God never requires anything of you that you cannot do. Without the love of God dwelling in your heart you couldn't continually love as God is asking you to do.[39] In your possession is everything you need to obey all of God's commands.[40] Not only are we to love those that hate us, but Jesus takes it a step further when He teaches on the topic of reconciliation, or repairing relationships. He said when you come to the altar to bring your gift and you know your brother has an ought against you, leave your gift and first be reconciled with your brother. After that is done, come and offer your gift unto the Lord.[41] Humility is needed when you have to go and be reconciled to someone who has a problem with you. The natural man would love to say "Oh well, that's their problem, not mine!" That's the wrong attitude to have. If there is something you can say or do to help your brother work through their offense, you should be willing to do it. It takes a heart of compassion and humility to drop your plans and agenda (leave your gift at the altar) and go to your brother, who perhaps may have no intention of coming to you.

Jesus demonstrated a very practical lesson on the topic of humility when He washed the feet of His disciples.[42] Peter was the only disciple who expressed any objections. He initially forbade Jesus from washing his feet. He looked at the task at face value and felt that his teacher, the Messiah, should not be lowering Himself to wash feet. Jesus turned this into a great teachable moment. Jesus explained that even though He was both Master and Lord, He was not too great to serve in such a humbling manner; furthermore, He expected them to do the same.

You may be willing to wash the feet of a friend or another born-again believer, but what about your enemy? Jesus knew that Judas would betray Him yet He washed his feet too. It takes a great measure of humility to serve your enemy with the right spirit and attitude. Jesus loved all of the disciples, including Judas; but that does not mean He did not feel the pain of betrayal.[43] The disciples would soon find out about Judas, consequently, Jesus gives the command to love each other as He has loved them.[44] That command is extended to the modern day disciples of this present time as well. "By this shall all men know that you are my disciples, if you have love one to another (John 13:35)." As a disciple of Christ, you are commanded to love. It has to be the same unconditional love found in 1 Corinthians 13; this love "is not conceited (arrogant and inflated with pride); it is not rude (unmannerly) and does not act unbecomingly. Love (God's love in us) does not insist on its own rights or its own way, for it is not self-seeking; it is not touchy or fretful or resentful; it takes no account of the evil done to it [it pays no attention to a suffered wrong] (1 Cor. 13:5, AMP)."

Humility is not a life principle that can be learned quickly by simply reading or attending a class or two. Although the disciples heard Jesus teach on the subject, they struggled with the concept. In Mark 9, the disciples were arguing among themselves as to who should be the greatest (v. 34). On another occasion, while teaching, Jesus reminded the disciples, as well as the multitude, "He that is greatest among you shall be your servant (Matt. 23:11)." Service to God can never be about seeking status in the Kingdom of God. You should regularly check your motive behind what you do for God. Some people serve for a set time in hopes of achieving a title, so the true motive behind their service is prideful. Once they achieve their title or desired status, they move beyond serving and actually want others to serve them. That is the mindset of the world and it is contrary to the attitude needed in the Kingdom of God. "Let this mind be in you which was also in Christ Jesus (Phil. 2:5)." Jesus maintained a mindset of humility at all times until the moment He died. Though He was God in the flesh, He took on the form of a servant, humbled Himself and became obedient unto His death on the cross.[45]

The Jews were no strangers to the topic of humility. They knew that pride and arrogance, total opposites of humility, were not acceptable in the eyesight of God. Throughout the Old Testament there are stories of those who suffered because of their failure to humble themselves in obedience and service to the True and Living God. Knowing truth and living according to that truth can be somewhat difficult at times. You can pretend to be humble in the presence of many people and perhaps even fool them into believing a lie, but God is Omniscient, all-knowing, and He can never be fooled. He always looks at the heart. He sees the very moment that a person wavers from a motive of humility to a motive of pride or arrogance.[46]

Humility is a choice and a mindset that each individual has to make on a daily basis. Humble yourselves under the mighty hand of God, that he may exalt you in due time (1 Pet. 5:6)." Each time the Bible mentions humility, it is always put on the Believer to do the work. Humility will lead to obedience, but pride produces disobedience. Fasting is one way to help keep your fleshly desires and motives under control and aligned with the Word of God. You deny yourself food, and perhaps also take a break from other pleasure activities in your life, and instead use that time to seek after God, praying and reading the Bible. You may also consider having an accountability partner(s) as you serve in the Kingdom of God.

Sometimes it takes another set of eyes to help you see yourself and keep your motives in check. You must be open to accept feedback and counsel, so choose someone wise, whom you trust and who will be honest and compassionate in their dealings with you.

Above all, God requires obedience from His disciples. Obedience to God's Word will often require a walk in humility, abandoning your own way of thinking and doing things. "I beseech you therefore, brethren, by the mercies of God, that ye present your bodies a living sacrifice, holy, acceptable unto God which is your reasonable service. And be not conformed to this world: but be ye transformed by the renewing of your mind, that ye may prove what is that good, and acceptable, and perfect will, of God (Rom. 12:1-2)."

Questions for discussion/reflection:

1. Re-examine the definition provided for "humble." What are some specific examples of how a person with a meek attitude would act, speak, and think?

2. What are some negative characteristic traits that prevent one from walking in humility?

Disciple's Discovery Scriptures

"Phase 5: Humility"

[38]Matt. 6:4	[39]Rom. 5:5	[40]2 Pet. 1:3
[41]Matt. 5:23-24	[42]John 13:12	[43]John13:21
[44]John 13:34	[45]Phil. 2:6-8	[46]Prov. 18:12

Phase 6: Authority

The final phase of discipleship is "Authority." This chapter was going to be entitled "Power and Authority." However, the more I studied, I saw that it could be summed up in one word. Power can be simply explained as "strength or ability to do something." Merriam-Webster defines authority as *"the right to give commands; the power to influence the behavior of others."* In other words, power is the ability to do something, while authority is the permission or right to use that power. Authority was strategically placed as the last phase.

If you fail to master the previous five phases discussed, relationship, discipline, stewardship, prayer and humility you will not be able to walk in the realm of authority that Christ has made possible for all of His disciples. Before you read about Jesus healing the sick, raising the dead, and casting out demons, read about His baptism and 40 day wilderness experience. He was the Son of God straight from heaven. If anyone could have been excused from wilderness training Jesus would have been the first choice, however, if He had been excluded, it would have disqualified Him from being a true example for us. Christ chose the route of humility to do the will of the Father, humbling Himself and being obedient unto death.[47] This was covered in the previous chapter on humility. The next verses will be discussed in this chapter: "Wherefore God also hath highly exalted him, and given him a name which is above every name: that at the name of Jesus every knee should bow...and that every tongue should confess that Jesus Christ is Lord, to the glory of God the Father (Phil. 2:10-11)." Because Jesus humbled himself and was obedient, God exalted Him, and gave Him a name so powerful that even to this day we experience and witness mighty works through the use of His name.

Jesus had to walk in humility. Not one time is mentioned where Jesus was bragging about being from heaven or telling everyone that He was the Son of God. He actually did just the opposite, including on one occasion secretly slipping away from the crowd of people that wanted to make Him a king.[48] Jesus was neither flattered, nor honored, because He knew His purpose and had a heart set on fulfilling His divine assignment. As He walked in humility and obedience to God, He operated in power and authority because of the Anointing, or the Spirit of God, that rested upon His life.

Jesus never operated independent of the Father and always remained under God's authority.[49] Others also recognized His power and authority. In Luke 7:2-10, a centurion (a Roman army officer), recognized that Jesus had authority over sickness and disease. He sent messengers to Jesus, saying he didn't feel worthy to have Jesus come under his roof. The centurion requested that Jesus pronounce healing over his servant from where He was standing. The centurion explained that he also was a man set under authority, and had soldiers underneath him who did whatever he commanded no questions asked. The centurion probably couldn't understand it fully but he had faith to know that if Jesus spoke the word to the sickness in the body of his servant, that sickness had to do whatever Jesus said, no questions asked! Jesus marveled at this man's faith saying, "I have not found so great a faith, no, not in Israel (Luke 7:9)." When the messengers returned to the centurion's house they found the servant who was sick, was now completely healed!

"Operating out of the authority of Christ comes at a cost."

Jesus lived a life subject to the authority of His Heavenly Father, and as a result, He was able to walk in authority while on the earth. Jesus taught with authority so much so that the people were "astonished at his doctrine."[50] He operated in authority over all demonic spirits. "And they were all amazed...for with authority commandeth he even the unclean spirits, and they do obey him (Mark 1:27)." Jesus was not limited in His God-given authority to just unclean spirits, sickness and disease. Jesus rebuked even the natural elements and spoke to a stormy sea. The wind stopped blowing and the sea became calm instantly! The disciples were amazed and asked one another "What manner of man is this, that even the wind and the sea obey him (Mark 4:41)?"

If you want to operate in authority you must first be subject to authority. The disciples were followers of Christ and got to the point where Jesus was able to send them out in teams of two and give them power over the works of the enemy. In Luke 10, the disciples came back rejoicing as they reported to Jesus that even the demons were subject to them through His name; yet, they did not have an all-access pass. Consider what happened right after Jesus' transfiguration. The disciples were not able to cast a demon out of a man's son. Jesus had to step in and cast the evil spirit out of the boy. The disciples asked Jesus why they could not do it and His response was "This kind can come forth by nothing, but by prayer and fasting (Mark 9:29)." This was the perfect learning experience to teach the disciples that true power and authority comes at a cost. Jesus was able to handle that spirit in the boy because of the relationship that He maintained with the Father which included regular fasting and prayer. Greater power and authority would require greater sacrifice and demonstrated commitment from them. You can see the new level of commitment and lifestyle change when the twelve disciples become the Apostles. The book of Acts tells of the prayer and fasting that took place on a regular basis, in addition to the miracles performed and the numerous souls that were saved.

In Luke 24, Jesus commissions the disciples to go preach the gospel to all nations. However, before they went out, Jesus told the disciples to "tarry in Jerusalem until they be endued with power from on high (Luke 24:49)." The disciples knew the gospel message, but they needed full power and authority if their ministry was to be effective. They went to Jerusalem as instructed and they tarried. They continued in prayer and supplication.[51] This eventually led to the day of Pentecost and the birth of the church. Throughout the remainder of the New Testament, we read about the powerful works of the Apostles and other disciples, submitted under and operating with the authority of Jesus Christ. As you read the book of Acts, you will see that the disciples experienced great persecution and adversity all for the name of Christ. In spite of the hardships and imprisonments, they remained prayerful, disciplined, and humbled as they carried out their service for the Lord. After being told to stop preaching about Jesus, Peter and John told the priests, rulers, and elders, "Do you think God wants us to obey you rather than him? We cannot stop telling about everything we have seen and heard (Acts 4:19-20, NLT)." The disciples knew that obedience to God must be their top priority at all times, chiefly because He was the Source of their power and authority. As they remained faithful in their relationship with the Lord, He remained faithful to strengthen and deliver them from the hands of the enemy. God's anointing increased upon their lives as the gospel was spread throughout the world and churches were established.

The Bible records what happens when you try to bypass God's process and try to do a work in the name of the Lord, without having a true relationship and God-given authority. You may end up in a similar state as the seven sons of Sceva in Acts chapter 19. The Bible refers to them as "vagabond Jews (v.13)." When used as an adjective, vagabond is defined as *"moving from place to place without a fixed home"* and/or one who is *"leading an unsettled, irresponsible, or disreputable life (Merriam-Webster, 2015)."* Scripture reveals that they were sons of the chief of the priests. They were more than likely raised in a spiritual home, knowing the word of God and the law. These men heard about what the Apostle Paul was doing and how evil spirits were being cast out so they thought they would try to do it. They "took upon them to call over them which had evil spirits (v.13)." Having no God-given authority and being under no authority they were powerless. These men were stripped of their clothing and beaten by the evil spirit. One can only hope they returned to their father's house and got back under authority.

Being submitted and obedient to God's authority is just the beginning. The Word of God instructs you to "obey them that have rule over you (Heb. 13:17)." These are people under whose authority you must submit, whether in church, at work, or out in the community. "Let everyone be subject to the governing authorities, for there is no authority except that which God has established. The authorities that exist have been established by God (Rom. 13:1, NIV)." You must remain submitted to the Spirit of God and obedient to the Word of God, if you expect to receive the results promised in God's Word. "Submit yourselves therefore to God. Resist the devil, and he will flee from you (James 4:7)." You want to have authority over the devil and every demonic force that comes against you. Operating out of the authority of Christ comes at a cost, which includes maintaining a close relationship with the Lord, living a disciplined life that lines up with the Word of God, and daily spending quality time in prayer.

The principle of stewardship is closely associated with the level of authority in which God will allow you to operate. As you prove yourself to be a committed, reliable, and obedient servant, God is able to entrust you with more responsibility and authority as you operate in His kingdom, doing all things for His glory.

This applies not only to the spiritual areas, it's the same in the natural areas of your life. The new person on the job, having the least amount of experience often starts at the bottom. They are able to work their way up to a management position, or a position of authority, after demonstrating that they are responsible, reliable, and willing to be accountable. This process takes time. This is common sense in the natural. If you want to operate out of the authority of Christ there is a process. There are no overnight wonders in the Kingdom of God. If anyone may have qualified to become an "over-night wonder" it would have been the Son of God, but even He had to go through a process. The disciples followed, served, and were taught by Jesus before He sent them out to do any type of ministry. They eventually got to the point where Jesus was able to entrust them with His authority. The process of following, serving, and learning is still necessary for all modern-day disciples. "Study and be eager and do your utmost to present yourself to God approved (tested by trial), a workman who has no cause to be ashamed, correctly analyzing and accurately dividing [rightly handling and skillfully teaching] the

Word of Truth (2 Tim. 2:15, AMP)." It's amazing to think that it all started with Jesus asking some fishermen to come follow Him and He promised to make them fishers of men. Ordinary people, just like you, were chosen for the extraordinary job of discipleship to positively impact the world through that powerful name Jesus. Now it is your turn to go out and impact the lives of those in your sphere of influence. Your personal relationship with Jesus Christ more than qualifies you for this assignment. "Behold, I give unto you power to tread on serpents and scorpions, and over all the power of the enemy: and nothing shall by any means hurt you (Luke 10:19)." God is with you every step of the way and help is only a prayer away. "Finally, my brethren, be strong in the Lord, and in the power of his might. Put on the whole armour of God, that ye may be able to stand against the wiles of the devil (Eph. 6:10-11)."

Questions for discussion/reflection:

1. **Re-read the story of the seven sons of Sceva in Acts 19:13-17. What lessons can be learned from their story?**

2. **The disciples daily followed, served, and were taught by Jesus. Who are you following, serving, and/or being taught by? How often?**

Disciple's Discovery Scriptures

"Phase 6: Authority"

[47]Phil. 2:8   [48]John 6:15   [49]John 8:28

[50]Matt. 7:28-29   [51]Acts 1:14

Conclusion

You were at one time strangers, alienated from the life of God; but now you are saved by grace through faith. After you decide to give your life over to the Lord, you become His disciple and you will immediately find yourself in the first phase: Relationship. Although the next phase is listed as being Discipline, your current life situation may require that you now work on your humility, which is Phase 5. These six phases are simply focalized areas of growth and development. While you remain on this earth, you will continuously work on each of the six phases. As you mature in Christ, the Lord will have you working on multiple phases at the same time. No one is perfect and you will continue to make mistakes until the day you die. Thankfully, God has made a way for you to repent and keep moving forward. In effort to learn from your mistakes and to do better in the future, you must be willing to make necessary changes. Let us review the six phases once more and come up with a game plan for success.

Phase 1: Relationship. Having a relationship with Jesus Christ is the most important decision that you will make in your life. Create a list of the positive relationships that you currently have with other born-again believers and come up with at least one way to strengthen those relationships. If you don't have many or any, reach out and make a connection with fellow believers. Most churches have many auxiliaries that promote fellowship and help build unity among believers. Ask the Lord to connect you with a believer who will help strengthen and encourage you on your journey of discipleship.

Phases 2 and 3, Discipline and Prayer, make quite a team. Being a disciple of Jesus and living a life that is pleasing to Him is going to require much discipline on your part. Prayer is your time to talk with the Lord, and also a time when you allow God to speak to you. He may choose that time to instruct, correct, and/or simply refresh you while you are in His presence. Set aside quality time for the Lord every day. Have a prepared place, free from distractions, where you can pray, read your bible, and sit quietly before the Lord.

Phase 4 is Stewardship. With all of the blessings that God freely bestows upon you (gifts, talents, and abilities) comes great responsibility and accountability. Take a moment to write down the gifts and talents that the Lord has given to you, and not just spiritual gifts, but natural talents such as cooking, great sense of humor, or being great at math. After you have identified your gifts/talents, write out specific ways you can help or serve someone else using your gifts.

As you work on the first four phases mentioned, you will experience growth that will help you to excel in the final two phases. Phase 5: Humility. Stay humble before the Lord and remember you have been saved to serve. Just in case you were not able to come up with any gifts or talents, you can use your time. Take some time out to help, listen, or simply encourage someone else, such as a stranger or a perhaps a co-worker that you see often but never have time to engage in conversation.

Lastly, Phase 6: Authority. God has equipped His modern day disciples with His power and authority. You can walk in authority as you stay humble and remain obedient to the Lord. Set aside certain times weekly or monthly for prayer and fasting. You are empowered to be His witnesses, to destroy all the works of the enemy, and to share the good news of the gospel.

About the Author

Rachel Armstead is an evangelist, teacher, singer and songwriter. She is an ordained Elder under King's Apostle Church World Ministries, and faithfully serves at her home church, Greater Miracle Ministries in Aliquippa, Pennsylvania. Rachel has been teaching the gospel for over 20 years. She is a firm supporter and advocate for education both spiritually and naturally. She holds a Master's Degree in Social Work and has been employed in the field for almost twenty years. Rachel currently teaches at the Miracle Ministries College of Theology, where she has taught for over seven years. Through her ministry, she strives to equip and encourage others so they can fulfill God's purpose for their life. Rachel has been gifted with a voice to sing and has traveled and ministered at numerous churches, ministries and venues through the years. She has a love for gospel music and will release her first CD project in 2016.

References

American Heritage Collegiate Dictionary, (1997). Boston: Houghton Mifflin.

Cambridge (Ed.). (n.d). Retrieved from the Cambridge Dictionaries Online: https://www.dictionary.cambridge.org

Merriam-Webster (Ed.).(n.d). Retrieved from Merriam-Webster Dictionary, Thesaurus, and Encyclopedia: https://www.merriam-webster.com

Prayer/Dictionary of Theology. (n.d.). Retrieved from CARM.org: https://carm.org/dictionary-prayer

Strong, J. (1890). Strong's Exhaustive Concordance of the Bible. Abington Press.

Made in the USA
San Bernardino, CA
21 February 2016